# BECOMING A
# CONTAGIOUS
# CHRISTIAN

## PARTICIPANT'S GUIDE

### REVISED AND UPDATED EDITION

# BECOMING A
# CONTAGIOUS
# CHRISTIAN

## PARTICIPANT'S GUIDE

### REVISED AND UPDATED EDITION

*Communicating Your Faith in a Style That Fits You*

## MARK MITTELBERG
## LEE STROBEL
## BILL HYBELS

*with contributions by*
**WENDY SEIDMAN** *and* **DON COUSINS**

ZONDERVAN.com/
AUTHORTRACKER
*follow your favorite authors*

We want to hear from you. Please send your comments about this book to us in care of zreview@zondervan.com. Thank you.

*Becoming a Contagious Christian Participant's Guide*
Copyright © 1995, 2007 by Willow Creek Community Church

Requests for information should be addressed to:

Zondervan, *Grand Rapids, Michigan 49530*

ISBN-10: 0-310-25787-5
ISBN-13: 978-0-310-25787-5

*Interior design by Mark Sheeres*

*Printed in the United States of America*

11 12 13 14 • 23 22 21 20 19 18 17 16 15 14 13 12 11

To the followers of Christ all over the world
who will confidently and compassionately reach
out to family, friends, and strangers with the
gospel message, which is "the power of God for the
salvation of everyone who believes...."

# CONTENTS

# ACKNOWLEDGMENTS

The authors express their sincere appreciation to:

- The people of Willow Creek Community Church in suburban Chicago, where this project originated years ago, and where thousands have been both trained and reached.

- Jim Mellado, Nancy Raney, Christine Anderson, Doug Yonamine, Stephanie Oakley, and the entire Willow Creek Association publishing team for facilitating the publishing process and for your encouragement along the way.

- Wendy Seidman, Willow Creek Association's training guru, for your extra efforts in updating and improving this course for the next big run.

- Don Cousins, whose early influence on this project shaped it in significant ways.

- And to Garry Poole, Judson Poling, Karl and Barbara Singer, Kevin and Sherry Harney, Brad Mitchell, Laura Dorans, Paul Braoudakis, Steve Bell, Andy Cook, Gary Schwammlein, Jim Becks, Dave "Supe" Wright, Graeme Paris, Jason and Rachel Lane, Larry and Rosemary Estry, Dave Moore, Rick Richardson, Mark Miller, Rickey Bolden, Beth and Larry Dahlenburg, Russ Robinson, Nancy Grisham, Courtney Stevens, Lynn Norum, Joe Sherman, Doug Martinez, Julie Harney, Marie Little, Chad Meister, Jim Russell, Tom Chapin, and everyone else whose names we should have mentioned, and especially our own families—thank you for the ways you've encouraged and supported this kingdom venture. We appreciate you all.

Also, deep appreciation to:

- John Raymond and Zondervan, for your partnership in producing and distributing the original and now this updated course for use by churches and ministries around the world.

- And to the following ministries: CCN (Church Communication Network—especially Bill Dallas, Jay Mitchell, and Ryan Erps); Outreach, Inc. (especially Scott and Susan Evans, Ron Forseth, Lynne Marian, Jennifer Dion, Paul Pickard, and Kim Levings); the Luis Palau Evangelistic Association (especially Luis and Kevin Palau and Alan Hotchkiss); International Bible Society (especially Tom Youngblood); the Billy Graham Center in Wheaton (especially Lon Allison); and Mission America (especially Paul Cedar and Jim Overholt) for all of the significant ways you've partnered with us for evangelistic and ministry purposes.

# INTRODUCTION

## 1995

The *Becoming a Contagious Christian* course is designed to help everyday Christians—like you and me—to confidently and effectively spread their faith to people they know. The emphasis is on natural approaches that work over time to bring family members, friends, coworkers, and neighbors to the point of trusting in Christ.

If you are someone who thinks relational evangelism is very important but "it's not really my area," then we want you to know that this course is *especially* for you. We are convinced that, as you move through these sessions, you will sense a growing excitement about how God can prepare and use *you* to impact the lives of others for eternity.

Through a variety of formats including video vignettes, group discussions, role playing, and teaching segments, you will learn how to communicate the message of Christ in your own personal, God-given style. As you gain confidence and begin to put into action what you have learned, you will discover what thousands of people who have taken this training before you have found out: becoming a contagious Christian is an unparalleled adventure!

You will have the thrill of sensing the Holy Spirit work through you as you build strategic relationships, raise spiritual topics of conversation, express what God has done for you, and encourage your friends toward commitment. When God uses you as part of the team that leads someone across the line of faith, *watch out!* You will never be the same again. You will experience the exhilaration that comes with knowing you have played a key role in fulfilling God's central purpose on earth — "to seek and to save what was lost."

So get ready, roll up your sleeves, and let the adventure begin!

*Mark Mittelberg*
South Barrington, Illinois

## 2007

It's hard to believe that it's been more than a decade and over a million people trained since we first introduced this course. But along the way we've learned a lot about equipping Christians — especially those who are convinced that evangelism is *not* for them — to naturally and effectively communicate their faith. We've applied those lessons to this revised and updated edition. Our prayer is that it will serve you and the people in your group well, and that as a result God will use you to reach many more for him.

Your partner in the gospel,

*Mark Mittelberg*
Trabuco Canyon, California

# THE **BENEFITS** OF **BECOMING** A **CONTAGIOUS CHRISTIAN**

"Front line" ministries - List.

## Who Is Jesus?

 **DVD:** *Who Is Jesus?*

Notes: Savior, father, friend an intimate
relationship c him our Father.

To the world - unknown

An intimacy c Jesus is what God desires.

Luke 19:10 "for the Son of Man has come
to seek and to save that which is lost."
John 20:21 as Father has sent me I
Shall seek you.

Acts 1:8

## The Goal of This Course

> To prepare us to be contagious Christians
> who are active in leading others to Christ.

*For the Son of Man came to seek and to save what was lost* (Luke 19:10).

*As the Father has sent me, I am sending you* (John 20:21).

*You will be my witnesses in Jerusalem, and in all Judea and Samaria, and to the ends of the earth* (Acts 1:8).

## The Benefits of Becoming a Contagious Christian

 **DVD:** *Stories of Contagious Christians*

---

**Notes:**

Perception - peoples perceptions of
evangelism and Christ

Ephesians 6: 10 -13 suit up, "the whole
armor of God"
14-17 Breast Plate of Right-
eousness from God; teach me in your way
Lord. Shield of Faith. Helmet of
Knowledge. We need to Read
the bible to get to know the
word + to know the truth.

Suit
up in
the
strength
of the
Lord.

---

Sin is not good for anyone but when we do let the lord examine my heart by confessing to him.

When we help people find the forgiveness and leadership of Jesus, what are the benefits to us, to others, and to God?

Write down a few responses to each of these three areas of benefits.

■ To us?

Come to the Lord and let him examine my heart as I practice to your faith.

■ To others?

■ To God?

## The Problem of Perceptions

| Evangelism | |
|---|---|
| Negative | Positive |
| • Not a real person<br>• Ø such higher power<br>• You do have to go to church to be a Christian<br>• judging, hipocritical hdy Roller, | We have the freedom in this country to share our faith.<br><br>To share our calling from Jesus. |

# Components of Contagious Christianity

Contagious Christianity is fueled by *love*.

It flows out of _____.

It's built on *relationships*.

It's expressed in both *actions and* _____.

> *And how can they believe in him if they have never heard about him? And how can they hear about him unless someone tells them?* (Romans 10:14, NLT).

## It is a *process*.

> *My job was to plant the seed in your hearts, and Apollos watered it, but it was God, not we, who made it grow* (1 Corinthians 3:6, NLT).

## It's always a *partnership*.

> *Who is Apollos, and who is Paul, that we should be the cause of such quarrels? Why, we're only servants. Through us God caused you to believe. Each of us did the work the Lord gave us* (1 Corinthians 3:5, NLT).

> A person's coming to Christ is like a chain with many links.... There are many influences and conversations that precede a person's decision to convert to Christ. I know the joy of being the first link at times, a middle link usually, and occasionally the last link. God has not called me to only be the last link.*
>
> CLIFFE KNECHTLE, author, speaker, and evangelist

---

* Cliffe Knechtle, *Give Me an Answer*, InterVarsity Press, 1986.

**Individual Activity:** *Begin a Prayer List and an Impact List*

Turn to the last page and the inside back cover.

*Ephesians 6:18*

 **Groups:** *Praying for the People on Your Impact List*

### Directions

1. Pair up with someone near you, introduce yourselves if you don't already know each other, and share the first name of the person you wrote down on your *Impact List,* and what your relationship to them is (coworker, sister, brother-in-law, spouse, neighbor, parent, etc.).

2. Take a few minutes to pray together for the people you've both mentioned. To help you know how to pray, follow the simple prayer guide on the right side of the *Prayer List* on the last page of your Participant's Guide.

## Recommended Reading

Read chapters 1 – 3 of the companion book for this course, also called *Becoming a Contagious Christian.* These chapters are filled with additional information and exciting real-life stories.

BECOMING A
**CONTAGIOUS**
CHRISTIAN

BILL HYBELS
MARK MITTELBERG

# BEING YOURSELF –
## AND IMPACTING OTHERS

 **Individual Activity:**
*Styles Questionnaire*

### Directions

1. Read each of the 36 statements on pages 20–23 and record a number by each that reflects the degree to which you think that statement fits you. Your choices are from 1 to 5, with 1 being the lowest match to who you are, and 5 the highest. Here's a description of what each number means:

> 5 . . . . . . . . . . . . . . . . . . That's totally me
> 4 . . . . . . . . . . . . . . . Pretty much like me
> 3 . . . . . . . . . . . . . . . .Somewhat like me
> 2 . . . . . . . . . . . . . . . . . . . A little like me
> 1 . . . . . . . . . . . . . . . That's not me at all

2. Transfer those numbers to the grid at the bottom of page 23 and total each column.

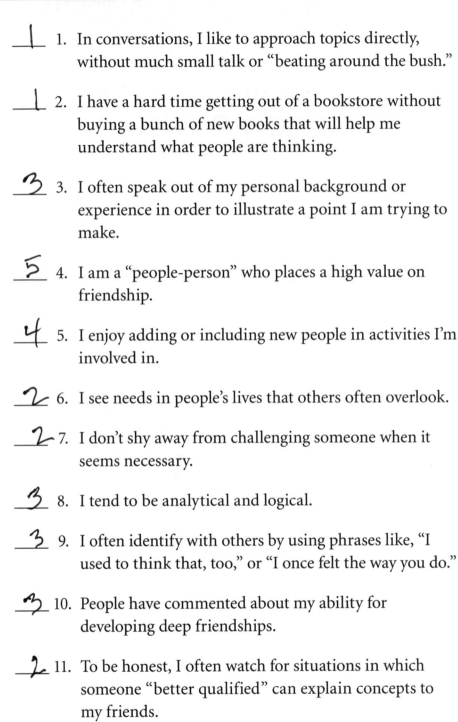

__1__ 1. In conversations, I like to approach topics directly, without much small talk or "beating around the bush."

__1__ 2. I have a hard time getting out of a bookstore without buying a bunch of new books that will help me understand what people are thinking.

__3__ 3. I often speak out of my personal background or experience in order to illustrate a point I am trying to make.

__5__ 4. I am a "people-person" who places a high value on friendship.

__4__ 5. I enjoy adding or including new people in activities I'm involved in.

__2__ 6. I see needs in people's lives that others often overlook.

__2__ 7. I don't shy away from challenging someone when it seems necessary.

__3__ 8. I tend to be analytical and logical.

__3__ 9. I often identify with others by using phrases like, "I used to think that, too," or "I once felt the way you do."

__3__ 10. People have commented about my ability for developing deep friendships.

__2__ 11. To be honest, I often watch for situations in which someone "better qualified" can explain concepts to my friends.

_3_ 12. I find fulfillment in helping others, often in behind-the-scenes ways.

_2_ 13. I do not have a problem confronting my friends with the truth even if it strains the relationship.

_3_ 14. In conversations, I naturally key in on questions that are holding up a person's understanding or progress.

_1_ 15. When I talk around the locker room or the drinking fountain, people really listen.

_2_ 16. I would rather delve into personal life issues than abstract theoretical ideas.

_2_ 17. It is not unusual for me to attend special events or concerts and bring along a carful of friends.

_3_ 18. I would rather show love through actions than through words.

_1_ 19. I think the world would be a lot better place if people would stop being so sensitive about everything and just speak the truth!

_1_ 20. I enjoy discussions and debates on difficult questions.

_4_ 21. I intentionally share my mistakes and struggles with others when it will help them consider solutions that could help them.

_3_ 22. I prefer discussing a person's life before getting into the details of their beliefs and opinions.

_1_ 23. I tend to watch for worthwhile events to bring people to (such as enriching seminars, retreats, classes, or church services).

_3_ 24. I have found that my quiet demonstrations of love and care sometimes help people open up and become more receptive to what I think.

_4_ 25. A motto that would fit me is: "Make a difference or a mess, but *do* something."

_2_ 26. Often when listening to teachers or TV commentators, I mentally (or even verbally) argue with their positions and logic.

_3_ 27. People seem interested in hearing stories about things that have happened in my life.

_3_ 28. I enjoy long talks with friends, and it doesn't matter much where we are or where we're going.

_1_ 29. I am always looking for a match between the needs and interests of my friends and various books, classes, and programs that they would enjoy or benefit from.

_4_ 30. I think the world would be a better place if people would talk less and take more action on behalf of their friends and neighbors.

_1_ 31. I sometimes get in trouble for lacking gentleness and sensitivity in the way I interact with others.

_3_ 32. I like to get at the deeper reasons for opinions that people hold.

_3_ 33. I am still amazed at how God has worked in my life and I would like others to know about it.

_4_ 34. People generally consider me to be an interactive, sensitive, and caring kind of person.

_2_ 35. A highlight of my week is when I can take a guest with me to a helpful learning event, including church.

_3_ 36. I tend to be more practical and action-oriented than philosophical and idea-oriented.

| Direct | Intellectual | Testimonial | Interpersonal | Invitational | Serving |
|---|---|---|---|---|---|
| #1 _1_ | #2 _1_ | #3 _3_ | #4 _5_ | #5 _4_ | #6 _2_ |
| #7 _2_ | #8 _3_ | #9 _3_ | #10 _3_ | #11 _2_ | #12 _3_ |
| #13 _2_ | #14 _3_ | #15 _1_ | #16 _2_ | #17 _2_ | #18 _3_ |
| #19 _1_ | #20 _1_ | #21 _4_ | #22 _3_ | #23 _1_ | #24 _3_ |
| #25 _4_ | #26 _2_ | #27 _3_ | #28 _3_ | #29 _1_ | #30 _4_ |
| #31 _1_ | #32 _3_ | #33 _3_ | #34 _4_ | #35 _2_ | #36 _3_ |
| **TOTALS** 11 | 13 | 13 | 20 | 12 | 18 |

# Six Styles of Evangelism

## 1. The Direct Style

**Biblical example:** _Peter_ in Acts 2

Characteristics:

- Confident
- Assertive
- • to the point
- _all or nothing type of guy._

People who probably have this style:

## 2. The Intellectual Style

**Biblical example:** _Paul,_ in Acts 17

Characteristics:

- Inquisitive
- Analytical
- _Logical_

People who probably have this style: _are very important because of our inquisitive world_

24

### 3. The Testimonial Style

**Biblical example:** The ___Blind Man___ in John 9

Characteristics:

- Clear communicators

- Compelling storytellers

- ___Good Listeners___

People who probably have this style: _because you have to hear others testimony 1st_

### 4. The Interpersonal Style

**Biblical example:** ___Mathew___ in Luke 5:29

Characteristics:

_Mathew party to introduce them to christ_

- Relational warmth

- Conversational

- ___Frienship oriented___

People who probably have this style: _usually focusing on their needs + life._

### 5. The Invitational Style

**Biblical example:** The _Samaritan Woman_ in John 4

Characteristics:

- Hospitable

- Relational

- _Persuasive_

People who probably have this style: _She ran + told the town about Jesus_

### 6. The Serving Style

**Biblical example:** _Tabitha_ in Acts 9

Characteristics:

- Others-centered

- Work behind the scenes

- _Patient_

People who probably have this style:

_Tabitha She served the poor Love good works trust is built_

# Individual Activity:
## *Styles Affirmations*

### Directions

1. Based on your highest total from the *Styles Questionnaire* grid on page 23, locate your primary evangelism style in the *Styles Affirmations* section of this Participant's Guide, pages 28–39.

2. Read through the information for your primary evangelism style and check the boxes by any items you think apply to you. If you sense that this style is not particularly descriptive of you, look at the style that had the second highest total on your *Styles Questionnaire*. See if that seems to be a better match.

3. From that same information, identify one idea for developing your primary style that you think you could apply in your life, as well as one caution to watch out for. Circle or underline them.

## Direct Style

**Biblical Example:** Peter in Acts 2

**Theme Verse:** 2 Timothy 4:2

> *Preach the Word; be prepared in season and out of season; correct, rebuke and encourage—with great patience and careful instruction.*

### Traits

☐ Confident

☐ Bold

☐ Assertive

☐ Skips small talk, gets right to the point

☐ Has strong opinions and convictions

### Cautions

■ Be sure to seek God's wisdom so you will be appropriately sensitive and tactful.

■ Allow the Holy Spirit to restrain your desire to come on strong.

■ Avoid judging or laying guilt trips on others who approach evangelism with a different style.

## Suggestions for Using and Developing This Style

- Ask friends for feedback on whether or not you have the right balance of boldness and gentleness. Keep in mind Paul's phrase in Ephesians 4, "speaking the truth in love." Both truth and love are essential.

- Prepare yourself for situations where you will stand alone (read about Peter in Acts 2 and other Scripture). The nonbeliever you confront with the truth will sometimes feel uncomfortable. Even nonconfrontational Christians who are with you will sometimes feel that discomfort. That's okay. Under God's guidance, challenge people to trust and follow Christ, and he will use it.

- It is critical that you listen and value what others say before telling them what you think they need to hear.

- Team up with friends who have other styles that may be better matched to the personality of the person you hope to reach.

- Other: _____

# Intellectual Style

**Biblical Example:** Paul in Acts 17

**Theme Verse:** 2 Corinthians 10:5

> *We demolish arguments and every pretension that sets itself up against the knowledge of God, and we take captive every thought to make it obedient to Christ.*

## Traits

☐ Analytical

☐ Logical

☐ Inquisitive

☐ Likes to debate

☐ More concerned with what people think than how they feel

## Cautions

■ Avoid getting stuck on academic points, arguments, and hair-splitting points of evidence. These are mainly to clear the path back to the central gospel message.

■ Remember that attitude is as important as information. First Peter 3:15 says to have "gentleness and respect."

■ Avoid becoming argumentative.

## Suggestions for Using and Developing This Style

- Set time aside to study. This style, more than the others, relies on preparation. Take serious action on what it says in 1 Peter 3:15:

  *But in your hearts set apart Christ as Lord. Always be prepared to give an answer to everyone who asks you to give the reason for the hope that you have. But do this with gentleness and respect.*

- Avoid doing all your preparation in an academic vacuum. Get out and talk to others. Try out your arguments and answers on real people, and make refinements as needed.

- Develop your relational side. Talk to people about everyday events, and what is happening in their life and yours.

- Team up with friends who have other styles that may be better matched to the personality of the person you hope to reach.

- Other: _____

## Testimonial Style

**Biblical Example:** The blind man in John 9

**Theme Verse:** 1 John 1:3a

> *We proclaim to you what we have seen and heard, so that you also may have fellowship with us.*

**Traits**

☐ Clear communicator

☐ Good listener

☐ Vulnerable about your personal life, ups and downs

☐ Overwhelmed by the account of how God reached you

☐ See links between your experience and that of other people

**Cautions**

■ Be sure to relate your experience to the life of your friend. You need to first *listen* to them to be able to connect your story to their situation.

■ Do not stop with merely telling your story. Challenge them to consider how what you learned might apply to their life.

■ Don't downplay the value of your story because it seems too ordinary. Ordinary stories relate best to ordinary people!

## Suggestions for Using and Developing This Style

- Practice so you will be able to tell your story without hesitation.

- Keep Christ and the gospel message as the centerpiece of your story. This is an account of how he changed your life.

- Keep your story fresh by adding new and current illustrations from your ongoing walk with Christ.

- Team up with friends who have other styles that may be better matched to the personality of the person you hope to reach.

- Other: _____

## Interpersonal Style

**Biblical Example:** Matthew in Luke 5:29

**Theme Verse:** 1 Corinthians 9:22b (NLT)

> *I try to find common ground with everyone so that I might bring them to Christ.*

### Traits

- ☐ Relationally warm

- ☐ Conversational

- ☐ Compassionate

- ☐ Friendship-oriented

- ☐ Focuses on people and their needs

### Cautions

- ■ Beware of valuing friendship over truth. Telling people they are sinners in need of a savior will test relationships.

- ■ Do not get so involved in the process of building friendships that you forget the ultimate goal: bringing people to know Christ as forgiver and leader.

- ■ Don't get overwhelmed with the amount of needs your friends might have—do what you can and leave the rest to God.

## Suggestions for Using and Developing This Style

- Be patient. This style tends to work more gradually than others. Look and pray for opportunities to turn conversations toward spiritual matters.

- Continually create and plan opportunities to interact with friends and new people through social events, sports, etc. This will put you in a place where your style can flourish.

- Practice telling the gospel message so you will be prepared when the opportunity arises.

- Team up with friends who have other styles that may be better matched to the personality of the person you hope to reach.

- Other: _____

## ||| Invitational Style

**Biblical Example:** The woman at the well in John 4

**Theme Verse:** Luke 14:23

> *Then the master told his servant, "Go out to the roads and country lanes and make them come in, so that my house will be full."*

### Traits

☐ Hospitable

☐ Persuasive

☐ Enjoys meeting new people

☐ Enthusiastic

☐ Spiritually opportunistic

### Cautions

■ Don't let others do *all* the talking for you. Your friends and acquaintances need to hear how Christ influenced your life. In addition, they have questions you could answer concerning the implications of the gospel.

■ Carefully and prayerfully consider which events or church services you take people to. Look for ones that are clear with truth but sensitive to the needs of spiritual seekers.

■ Do not get discouraged if people refuse your invitation. Their refusal could be an opportunity for a spiritual conversation. Also, their "no" today may become a "yes" tomorrow.

## Suggestions for Using and Developing This Style

- When inviting people, try to get written details about the event into their hands (either preprinted or handwritten). Whenever appropriate, offer to pick them up and do something together before or after the event.

- At events, mentally put yourself in the place of the other person. Ask yourself if you were that person whether the event would relate to your concerns and mind-set. Reinforce the positive aspects to the person you invited.

- Offer constructive feedback to the event sponsors consisting of specific and realistic ways you think they could improve the event and make it more compelling to the people you bring.

- Team up with friends who have other styles that may be better matched to the personality of the person you hope to reach.

- Other: _____

# Serving Style

**Biblical Example:** Tabitha (Dorcas) in Acts 9

**Theme Verse:** Matthew 5:16 (NLT)

> *In the same way, let your good deeds shine out for all to see, so that everyone will praise your heavenly Father.*

## Traits

☐ Patient

☐ Others-centered

☐ Sees needs and finds joy in meeting them

☐ Shows love through action more than words

☐ Attaches value to even menial tasks

## Cautions

■ Remember that although "words are no substitute for actions," "actions are no substitute for words" either! In Romans 10:14 Paul says that we must verbally tell people about Christ. You can do this in many ways as you point to him as the central motivation for your acts of service.

■ Don't underestimate the value of your service. It is your style that will reach the hardest-to-reach people. Acts of loving service are hard to resist and difficult to argue with.

■ Be discerning as to how much you can do realistically, without depriving yourself or your family of needed care and attention.

## Suggestions for Using and Developing This Style

- Find creative ways to communicate the spiritual motivation behind the service you offer. It could be through a word, a card, or an invitation.

- Seek God daily for opportunities to serve others for eternal purposes. He will open your eyes to areas you might have missed. Be ready to follow his leadings, even if they seem a bit out of the ordinary.

- Be careful not to impose your service on others. Pray for wisdom so you will know where to invest your efforts in ways that will be strategic for the kingdom of God.

- Team up with friends who have other styles that may be better matched to the personality of the person you hope to reach.

- Other: _____

**Groups:**
*Sharing Styles Affirmations*

### Directions

1. Form groups of three people.

2. Based on our discussions in this session, the *Styles Questionnaire*, and the *Styles Affirmations* which you just read, tell the others in your group:

   ■ What you think your primary evangelism style is, and why it describes you

   ■ One caution you need to watch out for related to your style

   ■ One idea you could use to develop your style

3. Listen to the others in your group to get a better understanding of their styles, and be thinking of ways your style might work together with theirs to reach people in your lives.

Train: strategic Evangelism
Target + aim first.

**Individual Activity:**
*Update Impact List*

### Directions

1. Turn back to the *Impact List* on the inside back cover of your Participant's Guide.

2. In the upper right-hand corner, write down your Primary Style as well as one or two Secondary Styles. Take a moment to do that right now.

3. Make sure, if you haven't already, to write a name on the actual *Impact List*. This will be the person you'll focus your thoughts, prayers, and efforts on in the near term.

4. Under this person's name, where it says "Next Steps," write what you think they most need in order to move forward in their spiritual journey. Is it for you to simply spend time together to deepen the relationship? Is there a way you could naturally apply your evangelism style, or involve another Christian with a different style? Should you offer them a book or CD, or introduce them to a ministry that can help them take next steps forward?

## ||| Three Concluding Thoughts

1. God knew what he was doing when he

   _____!

2. God knew what he was doing when he put you in your circle of non-Christian friends.

3. God knew what he was doing when he put you in

   _____.

## Recommended Reading

From the companion book for this course, *Becoming a Contagious Christian*, read chapter 9, "Finding an Approach That Fits You." It will recap what we've discussed here and expand your understanding of your own evangelism style.

# DEEPENING YOUR RELATIONSHIPS AND CONVERSATIONS

## Building Relationships

If building authentic relationships provides the context in which we can best reach others for Christ, then where can we initiate these relationships? We'll look at three places:

**1. People we** ___already___ **know**

- Include them in activities we're already doing.

- Take an interest in what they're already doing.

  Turn to your *Impact List* and write down any ideas where it says "Things to Do Together."

- Throw a "Matthew Party."

**2. People we used to know**

**3. People we'd like to know**

Go where people are — including repeatedly visiting the same restaurants, gas stations, stores, etc. — to become a contagious

_____.

## Key Points on Relationships

Key points to keep in mind when building and deepening relationships:

- Let the Holy Spirit lead you.

- ~~Guide you~~ _Barleene listen_ → first!    *Book of Acts about Phillip*

- Mention spiritual matters early.

*Let the Holy Spirit guide us.*

## Starting Spiritual Conversations

Three approaches to starting spiritual conversations:

**1. Bridging**    *John chapter 4*

Turns the conversation by using the topic being discussed as a bridge to a related spiritual topic.

 **DVD:** *Bridging*

---

**Notes:** *The Holy Spirit is already working in our lives (within us) let it guide us.*

*Share the gospel first*

*Slow to speak, listen*

---

## 2. Questioning

This is similar to bridging, but instead of making statements, it evokes a response by asking a question.

## 3. Inviting

Turns the conversation toward spiritual topics by inviting our friend to a spiritually-oriented event or gathering we think they might relate to.

Regardless of their response, your invitation can naturally turn into a conversation about spiritual matters.

 **DVD:** *Inviting*

---

**Notes:**

We have to help others overcome these barriers that they have preventing them from coming to Christ.

---

## Individual Activity:
*Starting Spiritual Conversations*

### Directions

1. Glance through the three scenarios described on page 47.

2. Imagine you are spending time with the person on your *Impact List*. Choose the scenario that would most likely fit your interactions with that person.

3. Write down a couple ideas of things you could actually say to transition the conversation, using the Bridging, Questioning, or Inviting approaches. Write these in the box after the words, "You might say."

# Three Scenarios

| Scenario | Possible Transitions | |
|---|---|---|
| 1. You're out in nature talking to a friend, and you can't help noticing the beauty of the trees, the blue skies, and the sounds of the birds.<br><br>**Sample Transition:** "God must have quite an imagination to create all of this beauty." | You might say:<br><br>*How beautiful everything is + say the Lord did a great job creating all of beauty* | Other Ideas: |
| 2. You are talking with a work associate about an upcoming holiday like Christmas or Easter.<br><br>**Sample Transition:** "I'm curious, do you observe any family or religious traditions around the holiday?" | You might say:<br><br>*Do you celebrate the birth of Jesus @ Xmas + go to Xmas eve service.* | Other Ideas: |
| 3. You are with some friends talking about popular TV shows, movies, news programs, songs, or books.<br><br>**Sample Transition:** "Another song I enjoy on the radio is _____ by _____, a singer who is a Christian, and really has a lot to say." | You might say: | Other Ideas: |

**Individual Activity:**
*Update Impact List*

### Directions

1. Take a moment to review the transition statements you wrote down on page 47.

2. Then turn to your *Impact List* to write one or two ideas that might be effective in transitioning a conversation with your *Impact List* person (under "Possible Transition Statements"). This is not so you will become mechanical, but to help you think through some useful options ahead of time.

# Key Points on Spiritual Conversations

☐ **Take initiative.**

Too often we wait for others to initiate topics of conversation. Be willing to take the lead.

☐ **Talk to people one-on-one.**

As a general rule, we'll get a lot further in spiritual conversations if we talk to people one-on-one.

☐ **Engage in dialog — not monolog.**

Most people are open to our talking *with* them about spiritual matters — but they don't want us talking *at* them!

☐ **Present truth in doses.**

Ask God for wisdom and sensitivity to know how much to say, and when to back off and wait for another opportunity.

☐ **Make the most of split-second opportunities.**

These are the daily conversational turning points where we see an opportunity and ask ourselves, "Should I or shouldn't I?" — and the choice we make determines whether we ever talk about our faith and actually influence others for Christ!

## Recommended Reading

To reinforce your understanding of building relationships, read chapters 7 – 8 of the companion book, *Becoming a Contagious Christian*. Also, take a look at chapter 10, "Starting Spiritual Conversations," which lists more ideas for turning conversations toward matters of faith.

# TELLING YOUR STORY

*Testimoney*

## Your Story Matters

Your story really does matter. Here are three reasons why:

- Your friends will be interested.

- They'll be able to relate to it.

- Your story is hard to _____.

> The skeptic may deny your doctrine or attack your church, but he cannot honestly ignore the fact that your life has been changed.
> CHUCK SWINDOLL, *Come Before Winter*

## ⫶How to Organize Your Story

| PAUL'S STORY: THREE HANDLES | | |
|:---:|:---:|:---:|
| HANDLE 1 | HANDLE 2 | HANDLE 3 |
| BC | ✚ | AD |
| **Christ** | **Christ** | **Christ** |
| **Acts 26:4–11** | **Acts 26:12–18** | **Acts 26:19–23** |
| "I [did] all that was possible to oppose the name of Jesus ..." (v. 9) | "As I was on the road, I saw a light from heaven ... and I heard a voice ..." (vv. 13, 14) | "So then ... I was not disobedient to the vision from heaven ..." (v. 19) |

**Concluding Question:**

"Do you believe the prophets?" (v. 27)

**Unifying Theme:**

Paul's intense passion for serving God (first without Christ, then as his follower)

# Develop Your Story

## Six Questions

# FIRST HANDLE: BC—BEFORE CHRIST

### 1. What was your early spiritual background, and how did it affect you as you grew up—your feelings, attitudes, actions, and relationships?

*Examples:*

- Our family was superstitious. We based our beliefs on things like horoscopes, so I lacked any solid foundation for what to believe.
- My parents taught me that there was no God—so we thought we were on our own to figure out what our lives were all about and to decide right from wrong.
- I was from a religion that taught positive things about Jesus, but denied his claims to be God and the savior of the world.
- We were a religious family, but all I remember were the rituals and rules—so when I got away to school I rejected the whole thing and went my own way.

*If you became a Christian as a young child, you may not have any real BC background to talk about. So you might say something like this:*

- I grew up in a family where the Bible was taught, and can't remember ever not believing in God. So I grew up with sort of a simple belief in him.

---

**My Story (Question 1):** I did not enjoy Sunday School where we went when I was young. It seemed like it was mean I quit going.

---

*Story Tip*: Wisdom with _____

## 2. What caused you to begin to consider following Christ?

*Examples:*

- A friend at school was a Christian, and she challenged me to look into the evidence for Christianity.
- I reached the point where I'd hit bottom. I knew the only hope for me was God—so I cried out to him for help.
- I got to know this guy who was different—in a positive way—and I finally asked him why. He told me about his relationship with Jesus.

*If you came to Christ as a child, you might write something like:*

- Most of what I saw in my parents, teachers, and friends at church reinforced my confidence that what I was hearing about God was true.

**My Story (Question 2):** my life was going o where, ladies I worked с wen spiritual + Christians, they lead me to Christ + became baptisized

# MIDDLE HANDLE: ✝ MET CHRIST

### 3. What realization did you come to that finally motivated you to receive Christ?

*Examples:*

- After a long time of looking for help in the wrong places, I finally reached out to the God I sensed was there, and asked him to come and rescue me.

- My reading and interaction with Christians convinced me that the teachings of the Bible were true, and I just quit resisting.

- After years of spiritual ups and downs, I realized how foolish it was to keep trying to run my own life.

*If you came to Christ as a child, you might say something like:*

- I don't know exactly when it happened, but along the way I understood that Jesus died to pay for my sins. Even though I hadn't led a wildly rebellious life, I certainly knew I'd done things that needed forgiving.

**My Story (Question 3):** Life seemed to be very unforgiving and things were falling down around me so I ~~b~~ went back to ~~th~~ the house of the Lord for a support + feeling of being loved by Jesus and his followers

*Story Tip:* Use of _____

## 4. Specifically, *how* did you receive Christ?

*Story Tip*: Making it _____

*Examples:*

■ I was at a concert where a guy explained that it wasn't enough to believe Jesus died for my sins—we need to ask him to apply that payment to our lives. So I went and prayed with someone afterward, asking Jesus to forgive my sins and lead my life.

■ After years of loneliness I learned that God wants to walk with me throughout my life. So I asked him to remove my sins and to become my very best friend.

■ It was hard to admit it, but I concluded that Jesus really is the way, the life, and the truth—and I asked him to forgive my sins and to begin leading me.

*If you came to Christ as a child, you might say something like:*

■ Even though I was quite young, I gradually realized I had done things that needed God's forgiveness. I began trusting in him, and have been experiencing his forgiveness and leadership now for many years.

**My Story (Question 4):**

# THIRD HANDLE: AD — AFTER CHRIST

These answers should address the problem or situation mentioned in your answer to the first question.

## 5. How did your life begin to change after you trusted Christ?

*Examples:*

- It's hard to describe the difference God made in my life. It wasn't just external; it's like my heart was transformed. Overnight my desires began to change.

- I can hardly put into words the release I felt. I knew my sins had been forgiven, and it was a huge weight off my shoulders. For the first time I felt true joy.

- My life isn't perfect. I still do things I regret. But my overall course has turned from being self-centered, to really caring about God and the people in my life.

*If you came to faith as a child, the emphasis in these final questions should be on the difference Christ makes in your life compared to what it might have been like without him. This can be determined, more or less, by reflecting on times when you were not close to him, by considering areas of weakness, or perhaps by observing the lifestyles of old friends and classmates who didn't follow Christ. You might say something like:*

- Knowing Christ makes a difference every day of my life. I know myself well enough to realize the mess I'd be in if it weren't for God's guidance. And even with that I sometimes mess up. That's when I'm most thankful for his forgiveness and grace.

---

**My Story (Question 5):**

---

**6. What other benefits have you experienced since becoming a Christian? Especially think of ones that would best relate to the person on your *Impact List*.**

*Examples:*

- Following God has given me purpose—knowing I'm here for greater reasons than just working, eating, sleeping, and doing it all over again. God wants to use me.

- I used to live with fear and insecurity. While I still worry occasionally, that sense of despair has been replaced with a calm confidence that my life is in God's hands.

- God has replaced what I used to think of as fun in my life with a kind of joy and happiness that really lasts.

- I've always had good friendships, but never with the depth I've found in some of our church family. Those people are closer to me than any friend ever was before.

My Story (Question 6):

## Concluding Question

It's best to end your story with a concluding question or statement that requires a _____ from the other person.

Circle the following statement or question that seems most natural for you, or write your own.

- So, that's what happened to me. Can you relate to any of it?

- How about you—what's your spiritual background?

- Were you taught any of this growing up, or maybe I can ask, what do you believe?

- That's my spiritual story. I'd like to hear yours.

- Does it make any sense to you?

---

**My Concluding Question:**

---

## Unifying Theme

This is the central issue in each of our stories that illustrates the difference it's made to know and follow Christ.

---

**My Unifying Theme:**

---

*Story Tip*: Use of _____

 ## Individual Activity:
*Outline Your Story*

### Directions

1. Referring back to your responses to the six questions (pages 53–58), circle a few key words in each of your answers that will help you quickly see the big picture of your story.

2. Write the most important of those key words in the spaces provided under each question on page 61.

3. Then copy your Concluding Question and your Unifying Theme in the places marked for those at the bottom of that same page. That way you'll have the full outline all in one place.

## My Story: Three Handles

| HANDLE 1 | HANDLE 2 | HANDLE 3 |
|---|---|---|
| **BC**<br>**Before Christ** | ✟<br>**Met Christ** | **AD**<br>**After Christ** |
| **KEY WORDS**<br><br>Question 1:<br><br><br><br>Question 2: | **KEY WORDS**<br><br>Question 3:<br><br><br><br>Question 4: | **KEY WORDS**<br><br>Question 5:<br><br><br><br>Question 6: |

**Concluding Question:** (Paul's was "Do you believe the prophets?")

**Unifying Theme:** (Paul's was his intense passion for serving God)

 **DVD:** *Telling Your Story*

**Notes:**

 **Groups:**
*Telling Your Story*

### Directions

1. Get with a partner.

2. One of you tell your story, while the other listens and makes mental notes of anything that was unclear or perhaps could be worded more clearly. For the one telling your story, feel free to look at your "My Story" chart on page 61 with the key words written on it—although you may find you won't even need it! *Note: The listener needs to cooperate with the person telling his or her story.*

3. After the first person has told his or her story, the listener should provide some feedback on what worked well, and what areas might be made clearer.

4. Then trade places—the listener becomes the speaker, the speaker becomes the listener. Repeat the process.

*Story Tip*: Length and _____

*Final Story Tip*: Focus on your friend.

## Recommended Reading

We recommend reading chapters 4–6 in the *Becoming a Contagious Christian* book to further enhance what you've learned in this session. These chapters encourage us in the three characteristics that make our lives, as well as our stories, highly attractive: authenticity, compassion, and sacrifice.

# COMMUNICATING
# GOD'S MESSAGE

 **DVD:** *How Do You Get to Heaven?*

Notes:

# God's Message

## The Five-Second Gospel*

"God loves us,

we _____Blew_____ it,

Christ paid for it,

we must _Receive Him_."

# The Four Key Characters

## Character 1: God. "God loves us."

- God is **loving.**

  *God is love. Whoever lives in love lives in God, and God in him* (1 John 4:16b).

- God is **holy.**

  *And they were calling to one another: "Holy, holy, holy is the LORD Almighty; the whole earth is full of his glory"* (Isaiah 6:3).

- God is **just.**

  *The LORD is known by his justice* (Psalm 9:16a).

---

\* *The Five-Second Gospel* was created by author and teacher, Judson Poling. Used by permission.

## Character 2: Us. "We blew it."

Humans were originally created good, but we became **sinful.**

*For all have sinned and fall short of the glory of God* (Romans 3:23).

We deserve **death.**

*For the wages of sin is death* (Romans 6:23a).

We are spiritually **helpless.**

*All of us have become like one who is unclean, and all our righteous acts are like filthy rags* (Isaiah 64:6a).

## Character 3: Christ. "Christ paid for it."

Christ is **God**, who also became man.

*Christ Jesus: Who, being in very nature God, [was] made in human likeness* (Philippians 2:5b – 7b).

Christ died as our **substitute.**

*For Christ died for sins once for all, the righteous for the unrighteous, to bring you to God* (1 Peter 3:18a).

Christ offers his forgiveness as a **gift.**

*For it is by grace you have been saved, through faith—and this not from yourselves, it is the gift of God—not by works, so that no one can boast* (Ephesians 2:8 – 9).

## Character 4: You. "We must receive him."

We must **respond**.

> *Yet to all who received him, to those who believed in his name, he gave the right to become children of God* (John 1:12).

We receive him by asking Christ to be our **forgiver and leader**.

> *If we confess our sins, he is faithful and just and will forgive us our sins and purify us from all unrighteousness* (1 John 1:9).

> *But in your hearts set apart Christ as Lord* (1 Peter 3:15a).

The result of receiving him is our spiritual **transformation** by the Holy Spirit.

> *What this means is that those who become Christians become new persons. They are not the same anymore, for the old life is gone. A new life has begun!* (2 Corinthians 5:17, NLT).

## The Bridge Illustration*

| KEY CHARACTERS | NARRATIVE | PICTURE |
|---|---|---|
| GOD | **God loves us,** and he wants to have a relationship with us.<br><br>[Write "God" on one side and "us" on the other side.] | |
| US | However, **we blew it** by rebelling against him, and this broke off that relationship.<br><br>[Draw lines by both words to form walls on each side of a large chasm.]<br><br>Most of us are aware of this and do things to try to get back to God, but our efforts fail.<br><br>[Draw arrows going over the "Us" cliff; these represent our failing attempts to get back to God.]<br><br>Our sins have to be punished, and the penalty is spiritual death — which means separation from God for eternity in a place called hell. That's the predicament we're all in — and there's nothing we can do in our own strength to change it.<br><br>[Write the word "Death" at the bottom of the chasm.] | <br><br> |

ILLUSTRATION CONTINUED ON THE NEXT PAGE

---

* Adapted from *The Bridge*, © 1981 by the Navigators. Used by permission of NavPress. All rights reserved.

| | | |
|---|---|---|
| CHRIST | But there's good news: God did for us what we couldn't do for ourselves, by building a bridge back to himself.<br><br>[Draw a cross so it touches both sides of the chasm.]<br><br>How? **Christ paid for it** by dying for us on the cross as our substitute. He paid the spiritual death penalty that we owed, and he rose from the dead to give us his life.<br><br>[Cross out the word "Death" at the bottom of the chasm.] | <br><br> |
| YOU | It's not enough to just know this. **We must receive him** by admitting that we have sinned against him and by asking for his forgiveness and leadership.<br><br>[Draw a person on the left side of the chasm; then an arrow to the right side of the chasm; then a person on the right side of the chasm.]<br><br>Conclude by asking your friend where they think they are on the diagram. |  |

**Practice drawing The Bridge illustration here:**

 **DVD:** *The Bridge*

Notes:

## Groups:
*Practice The Bridge*

### Directions

1. Get into pairs.
2. Decide who will go first.
3. Try drawing and saying The Bridge illustration for each other.

---

**The Bridge**

# Three Other Gospel Illustrations

## 1. The Spiritual Equation*

This illustration draws directly on the words of John 1:12. It's especially helpful for religious people who think that merely agreeing with the right facts makes them a Christian.

> *To all who received him, to those who believed in his name, he gave the right to become children of God* (John 1:12).

This verse contains three operative verbs: *believe, receive,* and *become.* Put into a spiritual equation:

Believe + Receive = Become

- **Believe**

  It is important to **believe** the right things. The Bible presents certain truths that we need to understand and agree with.

- **Receive**

  It's not enough to just believe these things. The Bible says that "even the demons believe ... and shudder" (James 2:19).

  We need to act on what we believe and **receive** the forgiveness and life that Jesus offers.

---

* Adapted from *How to Give Away Your Faith* by Paul Little, second edition © 1988 by Marie Little. Used by permission of InterVarsity Press.

■ **Become**

When we sincerely believe in and receive Jesus' forgiveness and leadership, the Bible is clear that at that moment we are forgiven of all our sins and we ***become*** his adopted son or daughter.

End by saying: "It's Believe + Receive = Become. Where do you think you are in this spiritual equation?"

## 2. The Judge*

This illustration portrays God's justice in dealing with our sin, as well as his great love for us. Many people in our culture relate best to stories, and this one presents the truths they most need to hear concerning Jesus and his work as our substitute.

| Outline | |
|---|---|
| A woman broke the law, was caught, and the judge gave her a penalty she couldn't pay. | A young woman was arrested for breaking the law. She knew she'd been caught red-handed and couldn't deny her guilt, and later stood in front of a judge's bench and admitted what she had done. The man wearing the robe was a kind man, but he was also a just judge, and knew he couldn't let her off the hook. She had broken the law. So he gave her the penalty prescribed by the law, which meant the girl was required to pay a steep fine — one that she couldn't afford — or else end up in jail. |
| That judge then came to her side and paid the fine. | But then the man did an amazing thing. He stood up, took off his judge's robe, walked around to the front of the bench where the girl was standing, pulled out his wallet, and lovingly looked in her eyes as he handed her the money she needed to pay her entire fine. |

(continued)

---

* Adapted from *More Than a Carpenter* by Josh McDowell, © 1977, 114 – 115. Used by permission of Tyndale Publishers, Inc. All rights reserved.

| The Judge (continued) | |
|---|---|
| Why? She was his daughter! | Why did he do this? Because the woman was his own daughter! Being a good judge, he had to honor the law and impose the penalty. But being a loving father, he was willing to come to her side to pay the price on her behalf. |
| She now had a choice: humbly receive the gift or not? | But now the girl had a choice to make. Would she let go of her pride, and humbly reach out to receive her father's generous offer? Or would she insist on trying to prove she didn't need help from him or anyone else, and end up going to jail? |
| God is like the judge. He requires a steep penalty for sin — and paid it in Christ. | This story illustrates the situation between God and us. God is a holy and just judge who said, "You've broken my laws and sinned against me, and the penalty is death." But he is also like a loving father, who said, "I love you and will come down and pay the penalty myself," and then he took off his heavenly robe, came to earth in the person of Christ, and paid for our sins by dying on the cross. |
| Now we have a choice: will we humbly receive his gift or not? | Now we, too, have a choice to make: to humbly receive his payment, forgiveness, and leadership — or to reject his sacrifice and spend the rest of our lives, and eternities, trying to pay a debt we can never fully pay. |

## 3. Do vs. Done

This final illustration is helpful for people who think they need to do good works to try to earn their way into God's forgiveness and favor.

| Outline | |
|---|---|
| **Religion:**<br>–is spelled D-O<br>–trying to do enough to please God | A lot of people don't realize that there's a big difference between religion and Christianity — it's in how they're spelled! Religion is spelled "D–O" [it's helpful to actually write down the word, "DO"]. It consists of trying to do enough good things to earn our way back to God. |
| **The Problem:**<br>–never know if we've done enough<br>–the Bible says we never can do enough | The problem is we never know when we have done enough. More than that, the Bible makes it clear that we never can do enough. (Romans 3:23 says: "for all have sinned and fall short of the glory of God.") |
| **Christianity:**<br>–is spelled D-O-N-E<br>–Jesus did what we couldn't do. He lived a perfect life, and died to pay for our sins. | Christianity, on the other hand, is spelled "D–O–N–E" [if you're writing, add the letters "NE" to the end of "DO" — spelling DONE].<br><br>That's because Jesus has done for us what we could never do for ourselves. He lived the perfect life that we could never live. Then he died on the cross to pay for all of the sins we could never pay for, and he rose from the dead to offer us new life. |
| **Our Response:**<br>–Must receive what he has done — by asking for his forgiveness and leadership | But it is not enough to just know this. We have to receive him and what he has DONE for us. We do that by asking him for his forgiveness and leadership in our lives.<br><br>Does this make sense to you? Have you ever received what Jesus has done for you? |

## Individual Activity:
*Update Impact List*

Prayerfully consider and write down which gospel illustration you think would best fit your *Impact List* person (inside back cover), whether it's The Bridge, The Spiritual Equation, The Judge, or Do vs. Done.

## Groups:
*Practice Choice of Illustrations*

### Directions

1. Pair up with one other person, and briefly tell your partner your *Impact List* person's first name and the nature of your relationship (neighbor, coworker, relative, friend, etc.).

2. Present the illustration that you think your *Impact List* person will best relate to, and say it like you're actually talking to that person.

3. After the first person has presented an illustration, the listener should provide feedback on what worked well and what might be improved.

4. Then trade places and repeat these steps.

## Recommended Reading

For further clarity on using these and other illustrations, read chapters 11 – 12 in the *Becoming a Contagious Christian* book: "Making the Message Clear" and "Breaking the Barriers to Belief." These chapters will help you know how to navigate through some of the obstacles that might be keeping your friend from following Christ.

# HELPING FRIENDS CROSS
## THE **LINE** OF **FAITH**

**Questions and Answers**

## Redemptive Resources

- Books and Recordings

- Outreach Events

- Each Other

## Crossing the Line of Faith

**Five Elements**

1. Approaching the line

2. Checking _____

- Have you come to the point of _____ Christ, or are you still in the process of thinking it through?

- That's great ... where would you say you are in that process right now?

- Is there any reason you wouldn't want to ask Jesus for his forgiveness and leadership right now?

3. _____ in prayer.

- Ask for the **forgiveness** of Christ.
- Ask for the **leadership** of Christ.
- Give **thanks** for God's forgiveness and leadership.

4. Celebrate!

> *There is rejoicing in the presence of the angels of God over one sinner who repents* (Luke 15:10).

5. Point toward next steps.

- The importance of **praying daily**
- The need to regularly **read the Bible**
- The importance of **right relationships**—with other Christians, with a solid, Bible-teaching church, and with non-Christians they know and will want to try to reach for Christ.

For more information on how to help your new Christian friends get off on the right foot, see the section marked "Taking Next Steps of Faith" on pages 89–91 in the Appendix.

 **DVD:** *Crossing the Line*

Notes:

## Groups:
*Pray for Impact List Friends*

### Directions

1. Break into pairs in order to focus together one more time on the people in our lives who most need Christ.

2. Look at your *Impact List*, and tell each other what you think your next step needs to be to try to reach your *Impact List* person. (Optional: You may want to write it on your *Impact List* in the space provided at the bottom.)

3. Pray for each other, that God will lead, empower, and use both of you—and pray for the people on each of your lists, that God will draw them to himself, and open their eyes to their need for Christ.

## Recommended Reading

In order to expand your understanding and passion for leading friends to Christ, read the final section, chapters 13–15, of the companion book *Becoming a Contagious Christian*. It will deepen your understanding, and encourage you with great stories.

# APPENDIX

## COURSE EVALUATION

## Material

1. To what extent did this program meet your expectations in terms of value and quality?

| 5 | 4 | 3 | 2 | 1 |
|---|---|---|---|---|
| Went beyond expectations | | Met expectations | | Less than expected |

2. How much learning did you experience during this program?

| 5 | 4 | 3 | 2 | 1 |
|---|---|---|---|---|
| Significant | | Moderate | | Little |

3. How relevant is what you learned to your church or ministry?

| 5 | 4 | 3 | 2 | 1 |
|---|---|---|---|---|
| Highly relevant | | Somewhat relevant | | Not relevant |

4. Would you recommend that others attend this program?

| 5 | 4 | 3 | 2 | 1 |
|---|---|---|---|---|
| Yes definitely | | Possibly | | Definitely not |

5. What aspects of this program were most useful?

_____

_____

_____

6. What aspects of this program were least useful?

_____

_____

_____

7. What, if anything, should have been included that was not?

_____

_____

_____

## Instructor

8. To what extent did the instructor demonstrate depth of understanding and credibility with regard to the material?

| 5 | 4 | 3 | 2 | 1 |
|---|---|---|---|---|
| To a very great extent | | To some extent | | To little or no extent |

9. To what extent did the instructor have a motivating effect, contributing to your learning?

| 5 | 4 | 3 | 2 | 1 |
|---|---|---|---|---|
| To a very great extent | | To some extent | | To little or no extent |

10. To what extent did the instructor's interaction with the participants facilitate your learning?

| 5 | 4 | 3 | 2 | 1 |
|---|---|---|---|---|
| To a very great extent | | To some extent | | To little or no extent |

11. Comments:

_____

_____

_____

_____

_____

_____

## STYLES SURVEY

In order to help us stay in touch and be able to let you know about upcoming training and outreach opportunities related to your evangelism style, we'd like to have you fill out the following information and drop it off on your way out of the session today:

Name:


Primary Evangelism Style(s):


Secondary Evangelism Style(s):


Mailing Address:


Phone Number(s):


Email Address(es):


Thanks! We look forward to working together as "links in the chain" to reach out to people for Christ.

# TAKING NEXT STEPS OF FAITH

It would be easy to think of our friends' step of receiving Christ as an end, but it's not. It's really a beginning! As the Bible explains, it's their birth into a new life. This means that, spiritually, our friends are newborn babies who need immediate kinds of spiritual nourishment and support.

Within minutes or, at most, hours of their putting trust in Christ, we need to encourage and coach our new brothers and sisters in Christ so they get off on the right foot in their walk with God.

Here are five areas to cover as part of this orientation to spiritual health and growth:

## 1. Praying Daily

Explain the importance of setting aside at least a few minutes each day to connect with God. Encourage them to talk to God using ordinary language, and to be honest about what's really on their mind each day. Even if they don't feel like praying, that's a good thing to talk to God about!

To help gain balance in prayer, you might want to mention the classic A-C-T-S outline:

A—is for **adoration**: worshiping God

C—is for **confession**: admitting sins to God and receiving his forgiveness

**T** — is for **thanksgiving**: a natural response to his daily blessings

**S** — is for **supplication**: an older word that means to make requests to God

## 2. Read the Bible

Explain that the primary way God speaks to us is through the Bible. Encourage the habit, beginning right away, of reading a chapter each day. Suggest starting in one of the New Testament gospels, and reading from a version of the Bible they can understand. If they don't have one, that would be a great "spiritual birthday present" to give them! The "Recommended Resources" section lists a few good Bibles and books for new believers.

## 3. Right Relationships — with Other Christians

Stress the importance of developing growing friendships with other Christians, and regularly spending time with them, especially in smaller group settings. Those relationships will be an important source of encouragement, learning, and accountability — as well as friendship and fun!

Also, at least for the first stages of growth, as "spiritual babies" new believers will need someone who is committed to spiritually "parenting" and coaching them. This can be you, or another mature believer who has affinity with them (select a person of the same gender). Either option is fine, as long as we make certain someone owns the responsibility of walking our friends toward spiritual maturity. The crime we must never commit is abandoning a newborn spiritual baby!

## 4. Relationships — with a Church

Encourage attendance at a church that accurately teaches the Bible, and that encourages and fosters spiritual health and growth. New believers need to understand that the church is not only a place to learn and grow, but also a place where God wants to use us to serve others in ways that will bless and build them up. New Christians need to know they have a vital role in God's family!

## 5. Relationships — with Non-Christians

New believers need to understand that God also wants them to become contagious Christians who will be used to spread their faith to others. Share some of the principles you've learned about this, and encourage them to come through this training as well.

But caution them to be patient with close friends and family members. Friends and family will probably need time to see that the change in your friend's life is real before they'll consider the implications of the gospel for themselves. Remind new believers how long *they* took to step across the line of faith!

## ADDITIONAL GOSPEL ILLUSTRATIONS

## The Roman Road

Use this illustration with people who are open to looking at the Bible directly and considering its claims for themselves. Some people need to see the gospel explained in black and white in the Bible, and this is a good way to do that.

Each verse in the illustration — all from the book of Romans, hence the name — is followed by possible dialog you may have with your friend.

### Romans 3:23

*For all have sinned and fall short of the glory of God.*

The Bible tells us that *all* have fallen short. That certainly includes me. Would you agree that it also includes you?

### Romans 6:23

*For the wages of sin is death, but the gift of God is eternal life in Christ Jesus our Lord.*

We both just admitted that we have fallen short. This verse shows we are in a real predicament, because *the wages of sin is death*. In other words, this is what we have earned as a result of falling short.

The good news comes out in the second half of the verse. We do not have to suffer death on account of our sins, because *the gift of God is eternal life in Christ Jesus our Lord*. But it is not enough to just know this — we have to act.

**Romans 10:13**

*Everyone who calls on the name of the Lord will be saved.*

This verse shows that if we are willing to call on the name of the Lord, to accept Jesus as our forgiver and leader, then we will be saved.

Would you like to take this step?

**Tip**: Mark these verses in a small New Testament and "chain" them together. In the margin next to Romans 3:23, write "Romans 6:23," which will show that the next milestone in the road is Romans 6:23. Next to Romans 6:23, write "Romans 10:13." Keep this New Testament in reach for whenever you need it.

# Baseball

This illustration is effective with those who have misplaced confidence in religion, especially if the person is a sports fan. It fits well with the Do vs. Done and the Roman Road illustrations.

Earning our way into God's favor would be like a baseball player trying to get into an imaginary All-Universe Player's Association that requires a minimum twenty-year career batting average of 1000, with no errors. God's standard is like that, requiring us to always be doing everything God wants and never stepping outside the boundaries of his commands. Thankfully, that is exactly what Christ, our substitute ("designated hitter"), did for us, followed by dying to pay the full price for our shortcomings.

# Niagara Falls*

This is a good illustration for those who need a clearer picture of what real faith is. It also shows our helplessness without Christ.

This is about a man who was rolling a wheelbarrow back and forth across the Niagara River on a tightrope. Thousands of people on both banks cheered him on. Next he put a two-hundred pound sack of dirt in the wheelbarrow and rolled it across and back.

"Who believes I can roll a man across?" he asked. Everybody cheered and shouted their agreement. The tightrope walker then asked, "Who will come and sit in the wheelbarrow?"

The crowd grew entirely silent; nobody was willing to risk it. Although they professed belief, nobody was willing to act on it. And so it is with Christ.

# Swimming Across the Ocean

Use this illustration with anyone who struggles with self-righteousness, thinking their goodness will somehow get them back to God. This illustration is simple and clear.

Suppose we decided to swim across the ocean entirely unassisted. You might make it farther than me, and an Olympic Gold Medal swimmer would make it farther than either of us. The fact is that nobody can do it.

That's the way it is with trying to live up to God's standard. We all fall short (Romans 3:23). We all need help from God to make it, and it is Christ who makes it possible.

---

\* Adapted from *Peace with God*, Billy Graham, © 1953, 1984 by Billy Graham. Word Inc. All rights reserved.

# Marriage*

This is a good illustration for a religious person who "knows all about church and religion," but does not really know Christ.

A bachelor may say "Sure, I believe in marriage—I'm sold on it. You should see all the books I've read. I'm an expert on the subject. Besides, I've been to plenty of weddings. Funny thing though, I can't quite understand it. Marriage doesn't seem real to me."

Very simply, this person has not discovered that, to become married, a man first *believes* in a woman, then *receives* her into his life. To get married, one has to make a commitment and say, "I do," promising himself to the other person and establishing a relationship. This involves a total commitment.

While we may smile at this bachelor, some of us may be just like him. The parallel is obvious. Someone may "know" all about Jesus, but not know the Lord himself. Being a Christian requires committing ourselves to a living Lord.

# Airplane

This is a good one for the same person as the Marriage illustration—someone who needs to understand that, beyond having a right knowledge of the facts, a step of action is required.

We are often like the woman who wanted to fly to another city. She studied all about aviation, discovered which airline had the safest record, went to the airport, found the right flight, checked

---

* Adapted from *How to Give Away Your Faith*, Paul Little, second edition © 1988 by Marie Little. Used by permission of InterVarsity Press.

over the airplane, and even interviewed the pilot, only to stand on the runway and watch the plane take off without her.

Many people know all about the Bible, the gospel of Christ, and the forgiveness and new life available for the asking. But they never "get on board" by actually asking for and receiving what God has for them.

## School

Use this illustration with those who compare themselves to others and, because they consider themselves morally above average, believe they are okay. This illustration is especially well suited to students.

Many people assume that God is like their teachers in school who grade on a "curve." However, the Bible tells us that is a false hope. God is completely just and therefore must judge *all* sin, even "average" sin.

The good news is that, while God does not grade on a curve, he does something even better. He takes the test in our place—and he gets a perfect score! Jesus Christ did that by living a perfect life in our place, then dying to pay the penalty for our sins. Why not ask him to "apply his perfect score to your grade book" by asking him to forgive your sins?

## WRITE OUT YOUR STORY

_____

_____

_____

_____

_____

_____

_____

_____

_____

_____

_____

_____

_____

_____

_____

_____

_____

## Personal Evangelism *(to equip believers)*

*Becoming a Contagious Christian*, Bill Hybels and Mark Mittelberg, Zondervan, 1994 (this is the companion book to this course).

*Becoming a Contagious Christian Youth Edition* curriculum, Mark Mittelberg, Lee Strobel, Bill Hybels; revised and expanded for students by Bo Boshers, Zondervan, 2001.

*Conviértase en un Cristiano Contagioso (Becoming a Contagious Christian* book and curriculum are both available in Spanish), Zondervan/Vida, 2003.

*Building a Contagious Church: Revolutionizing the Way We View and Do Evangelism*, Mark Mittelberg, Zondervan, 2000.

*Just Walk Across the Room* book and church kit, Bill Hybels with Ashley Wiersma, Zondervan, 2006.

*Inside the Mind of Unchurched Harry & Mary*, Lee Strobel, Zondervan, 1993.

*Surviving a Spiritual Mismatch in Marriage*, Lee and Leslie Strobel, Zondervan, 2002.

*How To Give Away Your Faith*, Paul Little, InterVarsity Press, 1966.

*Out of the Saltshaker*, Rebecca Manley Pippert, InterVarsity, 1979.

*Evangelism Outside the Box*, Rick Richardson, InterVarsity, 2000.

*Conspiracy of Kindness*, Steve Sjogren, Vine Books, 2003.

## Resources for Spiritual Discussion Groups

*Seeker Small Groups: Engaging Spiritual Seekers in Life-Changing Discussions*, Garry Poole, Zondervan, 2003 (training/strategy for starting and hosting groups).

*Faith Under Fire* DVD small group curriculum, Lee Strobel and Garry Poole, Zondervan, 2005.

*The Alpha Course*, Alpha USA, New York (and Alpha UK, London).

*Tough Questions Series*, Garry Poole and Judson Poling, Zondervan, 1998.

*Reality Check* small group series, Mark Ashton, Zondervan, 2002.

*Why: 40 Days Pursuing Answers to Life's Biggest Questions*, church campaign, Mike Bodine, Dave Stroder, Ray Giunta, Paul Trainor, and Mark Whelchel, Pursuit, Inc., 2005.


## Resources for Seekers
### (to give to your seeking friends)

*The Journey: A Bible for the Spiritually Curious*, Zondervan, 1999.

*The Quest Study Bible*, Zondervan, 1994.

*The Case for Christ*, Lee Strobel, Zondervan, 1998.

*The Case for Faith*, Lee Strobel, Zondervan, 2000.

*The Case for a Creator*, Lee Strobel, Zondervan, 2004. (Also, the *Case* books by Lee Strobel are now available in Youth and Children's editions through Zondervan.)

*The Purpose-Driven® Life*, Rick Warren, Zondervan, 2002.

*Dinner with a Perfect Stranger*, David Gregory, WaterBrook, 2005.

*More Than a Carpenter*, Josh McDowell, Tyndale, 1977.

## Resources for New Believers *(to give to friends who recently trusted in Christ)*

*The Journey: A Bible for the Spiritually Curious*, Zondervan, 1999.

*New Believer's Bible*, edited by Greg Laurie, Tyndale, 1996.

*The Quest Study Bible*, Zondervan, 1994.

*NIV Study Bible* (New International Version), Zondervan, 1985.

*Finding a Church You Can Love and Loving the Church You've Found*, Kevin and Sherry Harney, Zondervan, 2003.

*Too Busy Not to Pray*, Bill Hybels, InterVarsity Press, 1988.

Prayer List:

Amelia
Elizab~~eth~~
Gordon
Wanda
Tie
 Bryant
Deb T.
LeaAnn
Bev
Dave
Louise + Ralph
 Stacey
Debra Jean

**WILLOW**
Willow Creek Association

# Willow Creek Association
## *Vision, Training, Resources for Prevailing Churches*

This resource was created to serve you and to help you build a local church that prevails. It is just one of many ministry tools that are part of the Willow Creek Resources® line, published by the Willow Creek Association together with Zondervan.

The Willow Creek Association (WCA) was created in 1992 to serve a rapidly growing number of churches from across the denominational spectrum that are committed to helping unchurched people become fully devoted followers of Christ. Membership in the WCA now numbers over 10,500 Member Churches worldwide from more than ninety denominations.

The Willow Creek Association links like-minded Christian leaders with each other and with strategic vision, training, and resources in order to help them build prevailing churches designed to reach their redemptive potential. Here are some of the ways the WCA does that.

- **A2: Building Prevailing Acts 2 Churches—Today**—an annual two-and-a-half day event, held at Willow Creek Community Church in South Barrington, Illinois, to explore strategies for building churches that reach out to seekers and build believers, and to discover new innovations and breakthroughs from Acts 2 churches around the country.

- **The Leadership Summit**—a once a year, two-and-a-half-day conference to envision and equip Christians with leadership gifts and responsibilities. Presented live at Willow Creek as well as via satellite broadcast to over one hundred locations across North America, this event is designed to increase the leadership effectiveness of pastors, ministry staff, volunteer church leaders, and Christians in the marketplace.

- **Ministry-Specific Conferences**—throughout each year the WCA hosts a variety of conferences and training events—both at Willow Creek's main campus and offsite, across the U.S., and around the world—targeting church leaders and volunteers in ministry-specific areas such as: evangelism, small groups, preaching and teaching, the arts, children, students, women, volunteers, stewardship, raising up resources, etc.

- **Willow Creek Resources®**—provides churches with trusted and field-tested ministry resources in such areas as leadership, evangelism, spiritual formation, spiritual gifts, small groups, stewardship, student ministry, children's ministry, the use of the arts-drama, media, contemporary music—and more.

- **WCA Member Benefits**—includes substantial discounts to WCA training events, a 20 percent discount on all Willow Creek Resources®, *Defining Moments* monthly audio journal for leaders, quarterly *Willow* magazine, access to a Members-Only section on WillowNet, monthly communications, and more. Member Churches also receive special discounts and premier services through WCA's growing number of ministry partners—Select Service Providers—and save an average of $500 annually depending on the level of engagement.

For specific information about WCA conferences, resources, membership, and other ministry services contact:

**Willow Creek Association**
P.O. Box 3188, Barrington, IL 60011-3188
Phone: 847-570-9812, Fax: 847-765-5046
www.willowcreek.com

# Building a Contagious Church

## Revolutionizing the Way We View and Do Evangelism

*Mark Mittelberg with contributions by Bill Hybels*

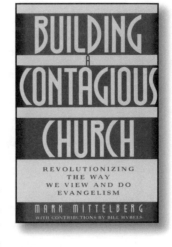

Evangelism. It's one of the highest values in the church. So why do so few churches put real time, money, and effort into it? Maybe it's because we don't understand the evangelistic potential of the church well enough to get excited about it.

*Building a Contagious Church* will change that.

This provocative book dispels outdated preconceptions and reveals evangelism as it really can be, radiant with the color and potential of the body of Christ and pulsing with the power of God. What's more, it walks you through a 6-Stage Process for taking your church beyond mere talk to infectious energy, action, and lasting commitment. Think it can't happen? Get ready for the surprise of your life! You and your church are about to become contagious!

Developed by one of today's foremost leaders, educators, and practitioners of evangelism—the principal author of the highly effective *Becoming a Contagious Christian* curriculum—this book's revolutionary insights have proved themselves time and again in all kinds of settings. So dare to get excited! This dynamic, highly adaptable approach is created to work not for some other church, but for your church.

Jacketed Hardcover: 0-310-22149-8

*Pick up a copy today at your favorite bookstore!*

# Becoming a Contagious Christian

*Bill Hybels and Mark Mittelberg*

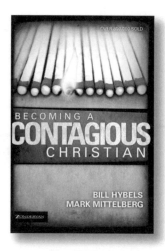

Evangelism doesn't have to be frustrating or intimidating. Bill Hybels and Mark Mittelberg believe that effectively communicating our faith in Christ should be the most natural thing in the world. We just need encouragement and direction. In *Becoming a Contagious Christian*, Hybels and Mittelberg articulate the central principles that have helped the believers at Willow Creek Community Church become a church known around the world for its outstanding outreach to unchurched people. Based on the words of Jesus and flowing from the firsthand experiences of the authors, *Becoming a Contagious Christian* is a groundbreaking, personalized approach to relational evangelism. You will discover your own natural evangelism style, how to develop a contagious Christian character, to build spiritually strategic relationships, to direct conversations toward matters of faith, and to share biblical truths in everyday language. This landmark book presents a blueprint for starting a spiritual epidemic of hope and enthusiasm for spreading the gospel.

Softcover: 0-310-21008-9

*Pick up a copy today at your favorite bookstore!*

# Becoming a Contagious Christian Youth Edition

## Communicating Your Faith in a Style That Fits You

*Mark Mittelberg, Lee Strobel, and Bill Hybels, revised and expanded for students by Bo Boshers*

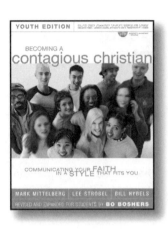

The bestselling *Becoming a Contagious Christian* training course—now revised and expanded for students!

For junior and senior high groups of any size:
- Small groups of 4 to 9
- Large groups of 10 to 150 and more

Can be presented in several formats:
- Eight 60-minute sessions
- Four 3-hour sessions
- One-, two-, or three-day retreats

After age nineteen the probability of a person accepting Christ as Savior is just 6 percent.

Think what that means for your youth ministry. Not only is today's greatest evangelistic opportunity as close as the relationships your students have with classmates, coworkers, friends, and family but the world's most passionate, effective evangelists are sitting right in front of you! No one can top your students in effectively introducing their friends and family to Christ. And now is the critical time to help them learn how.

Revised and expanded by one of America's foremost youth ministers and teachers, Bo Boshers, this exciting, highly interactive approach addresses the specific needs and challenges of students—in language they can relate to.

Help your students discover the evangelism style that fits them best . . . and watch them become truly contagious with their faith as they grow confident in introducing their friends to the love and truth of Christ.

*Becoming a Contagious Christian Youth Edition* Groupware kit includes:
- One 60-minute video
- Student's Guide
- Leader's Guide
- PowerPoint Presentation

All but PowerPoint Presentation also sold separately

Youth Curriculum: 0-310-23769-6

ZONDERVAN®
.com

WILLOW
Willow Creek Resources

# Conviértase en un Cristiano Contagioso

*Bill Hybels and Mark Mittelberg*

Evangelism does not need to be frustrating or intimidating. Bill Hybels and Mark Mittelberg believe in the effectiveness of communicating our faith in Christ. This should be shown in our daily lifestyle.

In *Becoming a Contagious Christian*, we will find principles that help the believers of Willow Creek reach those people that don't go to church and are ignorant of everything related to God. Based on the Word of God and on the experience of the authors, this book will give you strategies that will allow you to get closer to your friends as an evangelist and will help you:

- Discover a natural style for communicating your faith
- Develop a contagious Christian character
- Build strategic spiritual relationships
- Learn to direct conversations toward subjects of faith
- Share biblical truths in everyday language

*Becoming a Contagious Christian* will start a spiritual epidemic with the expectation of changing the way we communicate Jesus' evangelism.

Softcover: 0-8297-3857-6

*Pick up a copy today at your favorite bookstore!*

# Just Walk Across the Room

## Simple Steps Pointing People to Faith

*Bill Hybels*

What if you knew that by simply crossing the room and saying hello to someone, you could change that person's forever? Just a few steps to make an eternal difference. It has nothing to do with methods and everything to do with taking a genuine interest in another human being. All you need is a heart that's in tune with the Holy Spirit and a willingness to venture out of your "Circle of Comfort" and into another person's life.

*Just Walk Across the Room* brings personal evangelism into the twenty-first century. Building on the solid foundation laid in *Becoming a Contagious Christian*, Bill Hybels shows how you can participate in the model first set by Jesus, who stepped down from heaven 2,000 years ago to bring hope and redemption to broken people living in a fallen world. Now it's your turn. Your journey may not be as dramatic, but it can have a life-changing impact for someone standing a few steps away from you—and for you as well, as you learn the power of extending care, compassion, and inclusiveness under the guidance of the Holy Spirit.

The highest value in personal evangelism is cooperating with the Spirit, says Hybels. This means playing only the role you're meant to play—walking when the Spirit says to walk, talking when he says to talk, and falling silent when he suggests that you've said enough. Hybels encourages you to "live in 3D" . . .

Developing friendships

Discovering stories

Discerning appropriate next steps

. . . as a means of learning to understand the Holy Spirit's promptings. With fresh perspectives from his own reflections and experiences collected during his most recent decade of ministry, Bill Hybels shows with convincing and inspiring clarity the power of this personal, richly relational approach to evangelism.

Jacketed Hardcover: 0-310-26669-6
Curriculum Kit: 0-310-27172-X

# Seeker Small Groups

## Engaging Spiritual Seekers in Life-Changing Discussions

*Garry Poole*

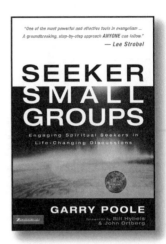

Principles and methods for effectively launching a seeker small group.

Bestselling author and evangelism expert Lee Strobel describes seeker small groups as "One of the most powerful and effective tools in evangelism." A seeker small group is facilitated by a Christian leader, but group members are seekers—non-Christians investigating Christianity. The group provides a safe context for seekers and believers to ask questions and dialogue about faith.

This highly transferable model can be implemented by all kinds of ministries with a wide range of evangelistic styles and strategies. As believers complete evangelism courses such as *Becoming a Contagious Christian*, they are motivated to reach out to others but often feel they lack opportunities to interact with non-Christians. *Seeker Small Groups* is the missing evangelism tool churches need to fill the gap between evangelism training and real-life opportunities for engaging seekers in life-changing spiritual discussions.

The book presents a detailed, step-by-step process for launching seeker small groups strategy in a wide variety of settings. The groups are for seekers whether or not they are attending church. Numerous stories and illustrations provide inspiration and encouragement so readers are not only equipped but also motivated to launch their own seeker groups.

Hardcover: 0-310-24233-9

*Pick up a copy today at your favorite bookstore!*

# PRAYER LIST

## People to Pray For

Ron

## For Your Friend

**Ask God to:**

- Open their eyes to the emptiness of life without him
- Help them see their need for his forgiveness
- Remove the confusion they have about him and the life he offers
- Help them grasp the meaning and importance of the cross of Christ
- Open their heart to God's love and truth, and draw them to himself

## For You

**Ask God to:**

- Help you live a consistent and attractive Christian life
- Make you authentic and honest as you deal with life's ups and downs
- Give you wisdom in knowing how to approach the relationship
- Expand your knowledge so you'll be ready to explain the gospel message
- Grant you an appropriate mix of persistence and patience
- Use you to soon lead this person to trust in Christ

## For Your Relationship with Each Other

**Ask God to:**

- Cause depth and trust to grow between you naturally
- Show you how you can best love and serve your friend
- Open doors for ongoing spiritual conversations
- Guide those conversations in frequency, depth, and content